100 Bars To Take You Far

All scriptures are taken from the Holy Bible, New King James Version®. Copyright © 1982 by Thomas Nelson. Used by permission. All rights reserved.

ISBN: 979-8-9996672-0-5

Copyright © 2025 by Perry Randle III, Vision Over Sight

All rights reserved. No part of this book may be reproduced or transmitted in any form or by any means, electronic or mechanical, including photocopying and recording, or by any information storage and retrieval system, without permission from the publisher.

This book is dedicated to my family. I would have NEVER made it this far without you.

CONTENTS

PREFACE 9

RELATIONSHIPS 15

MONEY 31

SUCCESS 45

HAPPINESS 73

EPILOGUE 97

ABOUT THE AUTHOR 99

100 BARS TO TAKE YOU FAR

PREFACE

Why haven't you moved on? There's nothing more frustrating than when something is stuck. Traffic, social media, food in your teeth–anything that refuses to move the way it should will get on your nerves. But what if YOU are the one who is stuck? That's the real reason you're feeling stagnant.

Here's the good news: you've picked up this book which means you still have hope to make it to the other side. And it is my pleasure to assist you on your journey.

You may not know what a "bar" is so let me help you. I'm not talking about where you get drinks, or a type of exam. *"That's a bar!"* is a phrase typically used when an artist cleverly packages words together to reach their targeted audience. This is usually done through alliteration, similes, metaphors and other literary devices.

> *"A bar is a clever way an artist packages words together to reach their targeted audience."*

You'll find a lot of rhymes in these pages but I am not related to Dr. Seuss, nor do I claim to be a hip-hop rapper. What I do understand is how powerful words can be when delivered effectively. Think about how you learned your ABCs, or the lyrics to your favorite song. You're more familiar with bars than you think you are.

The bars in this book will not solve your problems, but they will help you believe your problems can be solved. From the lowest of lows to the highest of highs, I can confirm saying and displaying these bars daily is what helped me move forward. Humbly speaking, persevering through hard times helped me work with billion-dollar companies before the age of 30. I'm not perfect, but these sayings have guided me on my road to success.

I'm going to keep it real with you though. Every bar in this book has come from—or been inspired by—somebody or something else. There's way too much history on this planet to pretend like either of us have never heard these sayings before. If this is your first time digesting this information, just know I've added my own flavor to each of these recipes that came before me. To name a few, here are my sources of inspiration:

- God
- Myles Munroe
- Dharius Daniels
- Jim Rohn
- Michael Todd
- Jermaine Cole
- Sean Anderson

Customize every principle to contribute to your calling. Do what works for you. If you don't like a bar, forget it. If another saying clicks for you, take it and run with it. I'm not here to waste your time. Each bar you read is designed to push you closer to your purpose. I can attest from my own experience that one bar can change your life.

Now that we've got the preface out the way, let's get to what you came here for.

Are you ready to make progress? Say less.

RELATIONSHIPS

The root word in "relationship" is relation. The Latin origin of "relation" comes from the word *"relationem"*. This means to "bring back, restore, or have a report". Everything we say, do and even think in relation to others will affect us at some point in our lives. We have to reframe how we approach connections because they are usually our reflections. Some people call it karma, while others refer to it as sowing and reaping. Regardless of how we phrase it, the golden rule of life remains the same. Do unto others as you would have them do unto you.

1. It takes one to know one

When I say this it's usually in a joking manner, but it has a lot of truth to it. The only reason you may be able to relate to someone is because you have probably walked a mile in their shoes. This realization often simplifies interpersonal communication. Similarities are some of the greatest sources of connection we have. Real will always recognize real, and harnessing vulnerability makes relationships easier to build.

2. If they don't know you personally, don't take it personal

As you spend each day at your job, you'll find this bar will be vital like no other. As a matter of fact, the same can be said on social media. There are many real and fake accounts that make comments without knowing anything about us. Don't get it twisted—it isn't easy ignoring people who are moving sleazy. But we still have to be cognizant of what we hear and read because it can plant the wrong seed. Filtering our emotions helps us respond effectively.

3. Lead by example, not explanation

You may have been around people who were in a position of leadership, but it never felt good to be led by them. And this isn't a slight, but it means there is a disconnect between the leader and receiver. It doesn't matter what their title is, a leader is someone who finds a way to inspire others to be the best version of themselves. So if you're in this position, remember the people around you are following your lead.

4. Criticism and compliments are two sides of the same coin

I hate to break it to you, but you aren't perfect and neither am I. This shouldn't be new information to anyone. As a man of faith, I believe there has only been one perfect human to walk this Earth and his name is Jesus. I don't know if you've ever read the Bible but here's a spoiler: He was crucified. So we would be naive and deceived to think people wouldn't love us one day and hate us the next. Whether someone is saying good or bad things about us, our job is to focus on giving them something to talk about.

5. Goals come with trolls

One thing we can count on as we pursue our goals is there will be an infinite amount of trolls. What do I mean by trolls? I mean there will be people that will try to pull us back down to the level we came from, or the level they're still stuck on. Every great person we admire had to overcome noise from the crowd. As the volume around you begins to increase, make sure your value doesn't decrease.

6. We have two ears and one mouth

Do you believe in coincidences? Because I don't. The word "coincidence" means to have two separate events agree at the same time. To think this is random or by happenstance almost seems foolish. And the way our bodies are designed often gives us hints on how we should handle them. Just like Dwayne "The Rock" Johnson, we tend to not be fond of people who can't realize when to know their role and shut their mouth. Instead, we appreciate being around people who are active listeners. We should spend our energy being the latter of the two. It's rare that the loudest person in the room is also the smartest.

7. The right mate is worth the wait

There is absolutely no reason to rush getting into a romantic relationship. It's in our best interest to enjoy being single as long as we can. And if you're not in the mood for romance, this still applies to waiting for the right business partner or best friend. The body is a temple, and the right people won't cultivate the wrong things inside of you. Wasted time, energy and money are some of the consequences of not waiting for the right mate. On the flip side, I guarantee from personal experience that patience along the way will reveal who to surround yourself with each day.

> *"The body is a temple, and the right people won't cultivate the wrong things inside of you."*

8. Separation sobers your situation

Life is all about the bigger picture. And this is hard to see when we are too close to what/who we are dealing with. Our feelings are valid, but they also vary. It wouldn't be wise to depend on emotions that are oftentimes fleeting. Let's take a step back, and write what we're feeling on a piece of paper. Read it aloud and if it sounds laughable, it probably means we're acting funny. Stepping away from our problems helps us get closer to the answer.

9. Help yourself by helping somebody else

Our energy goes up when our kindness does the same. I learned at an early age it is better to give than it is to receive. The feeling I get when I show love to someone and see a smile on their face? Priceless. Have you ever experienced this and unknowingly received the pick-me-up you were looking for all along? Remember this important lesson: having the heart of a servant positions you to be a king/queen.

10. Seeing it starts with you being it

Please remember outcomes change as soon as we do. You may want to look better in the mirror, but this requires you going to the gym or changing your eating habits. I might want a cleaner house, but this means I have to get out the cleaning supplies and start scrubbing. Don't waste your life waiting on someone or your situation to change. Become the change you want to see, and I'm sure it won't be long before the results follow your lead.

11. Leadership is more of a responsibility than a result

Make no mistake about it, everyone in a position of leadership isn't a leader. Why? Because a person with control doesn't mean he or she knows how to connect. They may hold a title, but they might not be all about the team. They can even be educated, and still not be effective. Being a leader isn't illustrated by displaying perfection. It means consistently empowering people who follow you, so they can learn from each mistake and become leaders themselves.

"Because a person with control doesn't mean he or she knows how to connect."

12. Not a bad tree, but it's bad for me

Dharius Daniels said this bar best. He elaborated by saying *"Everyone has equal value in God's eyes, but not everyone adds equal value to my life"*. This bar should help us refrain from judging others, and also have a honest review of whether a person is an asset or liability in our lives. Ask yourself, "Does he or she help me be a better me?". Ultimately this doesn't make them a bad person, but it may be time to look elsewhere when finding what and who works for you.

13. Pressure shows you who steps up and who switches up

Look at your inner circle, and go through the trenches of life with them if you haven't already. When these people show you who they really are, believe them. This is how you find out who is there for you all the time, and who is only there for a good time. Hang onto people who have your back no matter what season of life you are in, and reciprocate this energy back to them.

14. Know yourself so you can connect with everyone else

A lot of people suffer from imposter syndrome. This is a result of self-doubt, and also lacking the confidence to stay true to themselves. People will tell us who to be if we never show them who we are called to be. However, spending enough time alone will help us identify our unique characteristics. And any table we're meant to sit at will be OK with that.

15. It has to be by fruit, not force

If you're in a position of leadership, this bar is for you. Maybe the people on your team don't respond how you would like for them to. Unfortunately, trying to force them to listen is no fun for anyone. People following our lead becomes more likely when we focus on leading wisely. We can do this by practicing what we preach. Jesus is the greatest leader I know of, and He never forced anybody to follow Him.

16. Sharpening should lead to serving

We can go to school, seminars or any other type of class to carve our craft as much as we want to. But at some point we have to utilize our gifts for the betterment of others. Try not to get stuck in the cycle of learning without earning. Make it your life's mission to serve your talent to as many people as possible. You wouldn't be following the plan if your gift never leaves your hands. It's one thing to sharpen your pencil, but it's another to never write a single word.

> *"Make it your life's mission to serve your talent to as many people as possible."*

17. Work with people or else it won't work

We will not love every single one of our coworkers. And if you've already thought of someone specific, I know this person really gets on your nerves. But in order for everything to work out, we will have to work with the people around us. Chances are they won't be in our lives forever. Do your best to not be bothered by people who are here today and gone tomorrow. Trust me, it will all work out if we are willing to put the work in.

18. Experiencing the emotion is enough

BREAKING NEWS: we don't always have to relate in order to participate. Sometimes emotionally putting ourselves in other people's shoes is the most powerful step we can take. Even though there are different levels to each feeling, we've probably felt the same way in our own journeys to healing. When we allow ourselves to feel moved, our listening skills and conversation quality will improve.

19. Common sense ain't so common

I'll keep this one short and sweet. Whoever called it "common sense" probably didn't have it because it's a rare thing to find. And just like they don't know everything, neither do we. Flunking relationships solely because they don't fit our filter is a grave mistake to make. As we continue to experience life, we will see common sense will always be relative to the person who possesses it.

MONEY

Money is a common concept in our culture, but it can be difficult to define. It comes from the Latin word *"moneta"*, which can be understood as "a place (like a bank) where your funds turn into currency". Our financial situation is often correlated with our personal transformation. When we work on us, our money will work for us. We shouldn't lose ourselves trying to chase wealth. Doing this will put our growth behind a lock, instead of us using money to build our stock. Once we get the finances, do we still have fulfillment?

20. Wanna make it new? Just add you

There ain't nothing new under the sun. The only thing we have never seen before is today's date. This should simplify how we leave our imprints on society. Look at the greatest things people have done, and find a way to add your own spin to it. As I stated in the preface, all of these sayings were inspired by someone or something God placed in my life. However, my experiences allow me to deliver these bars in a way that no one else can. My advice to you is don't try to reinvent the wheel, but do your best not to steal because what lasts in the end is what's real.

21. All money isn't good money

None of us (especially me) sit on a seat that's high enough to look down on anybody. We can go to the extreme, and talk about illegal things people do to make ends meet. But there are still certain opportunities the law permits that we shouldn't accept. Why? Because making this type of money can cost us our peace, time, energy, you name it. Think of it like this: if an opportunity takes away anything essential to your existence, you will be happier existing without it.

22. Self-worth is never equal to net worth

Have you ever talked to a person and all they do is broadcast how much money they have, cars they own, blah blah blah… Well I have been on the wrong side of this conversation, and I'm 99% sure I blocked their phone number once the interaction was over. Materialistic possessions should not be the highlight of our lives. Take time to yourself to do inner work so everyone can see you for who you truly are. If we find our value in things that are tangible, it won't be long until we find ourselves in trouble. Your true worth can't be found in anything someone can take from you. Instead, we should wow people with who we are from the inside out.

> "Your true worth can't be found in anything someone can take from you."

23. Being cheap is expensive

We can still say no even if the price is low. Chances are high the product's quality will reveal if it was worth the buy. I know you love a good deal, and I do too. But we have to do our due diligence to make sure the deal is real. Oftentimes when we go the cheap route, we spend more money. There will be less of a fuss when we purchase the product that is most valuable to us. So how do we know what and what not to buy? Hint: always read before you sow your seed.

24. Learn more than you earn

Society tells us to chase the next dollar—and I'm guilty of this too. But my life changed when I decided to constantly seek wisdom from the right sources. Growing up, you could've called me a "happy fool" because I spent my direct deposit like it was burning a hole in my pocket. This could've been avoided if I created a plan for my paper. Being financially curious can help you have your cake and eat it too. One day you'll stop chasing money, and it'll start chasing you.

25. Impact over income

Even when life is going great, we shouldn't forget that we have an expiration date. I know that sounds a bit grim, but let me ease this thought into your mind. When you take your last breath, your money isn't going with you. I've never seen a U-Haul following a hearse. When people speak of you, you want them to mention the positive impact you made in their lives. Ironically, if we focus on making that impact while we're alive, it'll be easier to make a living too.

26. Time will never be equal to a dime

There's a saying that "time is money", and we often clock in to make money. But I'm here to debunk this myth. Every dollar you spend can be earned again. Time, however, is the most important non-renewable resource we have.

Every moment becomes a memory in a matter of seconds.

You've probably seen a dollar bill hundreds of times, but you will only experience this life one time.

"Time is the most important non-renewable resource we have."

27. Seek to serve, not to sell

If you work in sales, this bar should ring a few bells. We're all working for a paycheck, but the easiest way to earn one is by putting the customer first. Simply put, people want to know that you genuinely care about them. It only makes sense that a client will want to do business with you when they know you're doing the best business for them. Spend time finding their pain points and offer solutions. Your hard-earned money will be well deserved when you learn to serve well.

28. Retention follows attention

If you want the spotlight in your life, you can't be afraid of stepping into the light. Do you want millions of followers on social media? Post the content you haven't made, or whatever is saved in your drafts. How else will we find you and your gift? Be persistent and consistent with what you are selling. And this won't just gain an audience's attention, it will retain it. When we stop overthinking and produce, we finally put our God-given talents to use. Our followers will always want our content on their feed when we are fulfilling their need.

29. More of anything means more of everything

You've probably heard the song *"Mo' Money Mo' Problems"* by The Notorious B.I.G. If you haven't, that's okay–I'll break it down. All affluence comes with a nuisance. The new job you're hoping for? It'll probably come with an annoying coworker. Your dream house? It comes with a 30-year mortgage. And don't even get me started on a newborn–SHEESH. It's hard for me to keep it real sometimes, but I've got to tell you the truth. This bar is meant to prepare you for the burden that comes with the blessing.

30. You don't need to reinvent the wheel to make a mil'

Copy and paste is great, but you attract more eyes when you customize. Think about the businesses and people you interact with most. Jot down why you're invested in them: "I like [BLANK] because [BLANK] and it makes me feel [BLANK]." When you combine these details with your past, you begin to wrap a present for your future. There are always subtle details from our lives that hint at what we're supposed to do with them. And once you accomplish this feat, rinse and repeat.

31. Make availability your best ability

When seeking a new position, which skill do you highlight most often? If I were you, I would emphasize being someone who will consistently show up and show out as much as possible. Now don't get it twisted, I wholeheartedly understand how challenging it can be to achieve a work-life balance. But I also remember how hard it was to find a job when I didn't have one. When we're in the workplace, we should always say yes to doing our best. If you become someone businesses can count on, it'll be hard to ever count you out.

32. Numbers measure volume not value

It is more prevalent than ever to focus on analytics. There are a ridiculous amount of companies that obsess over metrics rather than the message. This is as backwards as pouring milk before adding in the cereal. Results take care of themselves when we think more relationally than numerically. There will always be somebody you can relate to and connect with. This becomes indescribably more significant than a fleeting number. So try not to get depressed thinking about digits. Remember that numbers never lie, but they often don't tell the whole truth.

> *"There will always be somebody you can relate to and connect with."*

33. Give your gift

When you receive a gift, it is often for you to enjoy. Ironically, the unique skill you are blessed with is for you to share with others. And whether we like it or not, there are countless times when we have to become a generous genius. This is a small price to pay in the grand scheme of things. Serving others for free will eventually help us earn a fee. We all want money, friends, and resources from sharing our expertise–but the true fulfillment comes when we touch others with our divine technique. So if you got it, give it.

SUCCESS

You want to be successful just like the majority of the world's population. But we all have our own definition when it comes to succeeding. So what is "success"? It can be defined as "a favorable or desirable outcome". Digging a little deeper into its origin, success comes from the Latin word *"succedere"*. I'll save you the research by letting you know its prefix "sub-" means "come after", while its suffix "-cedere" means "move". Simply put, we won't experience success if we are stuck. Whether it's in our mind or movement, we must go so we can grow.

34. You *should* do better when you know better

There is a significant difference between someone who is ignorant and someone who is foolish. The separator is called knowledge. Many people say *"knowledge is power"*, but I disagree. Knowledge alone doesn't guarantee growth. I can know everything, but if I'm unwilling to act, I'm just an over-motivated underachiever. It may sound harsh, but it's the ugly truth. This is why the word "should" is italicized in this bar. No one should fault you for the information you don't know. But once you become aware, it's time to throw some action in there.

35. Loss is a blessing if we learn the lesson

We will win and lose constantly in life. In fact, we might lose more than we win. But here's the thing: losses are as important as wins. We can try to avoid the valleys, but they are essential to us reaching the mountaintops. The best thing to do in any situation is to learn from the outcome. This will help us repeat our wins, and not make the same mistakes again. We need to find blessings in our downfalls, so we can see how necessary they are to our come ups (which means success or advancement).

36. Proper preparation prevents poor performance

I first heard this bar's alliteration from hip-hop rapper Big Sean. Our emotions often need to be disarmed before we perform. This doesn't mean everything will be perfect, but it does mean we can limit the improvisation needed for each instance. Performance anxiety can happen in sports, theater or even before having a tough conversation. The important takeaway from this bar is remembering what you practice privately usually shows up publicly.

37. Vision helps you make a decision

Studies show the average adult makes about 35,000 decisions in a day. Of course, most of these are subconscious and are often a part of our daily routines. But how many choices do we consciously wrestle with? Your thought process should be your tag team partner. For example, I LOVE snickerdoodle cookies. But if I'm trying to lose weight, sweets shouldn't touch my plate! We should always coincide our decisions with our visions. So when you are looking at options, always say no if a choice doesn't move you closer to your goal.

38. Keep the main thing the main thing

How draining is it when we find ourselves wasting time and energy on what isn't important to our lives? It's easy to get distracted by the small things. But in the end, they won't ever compare to the big things. When someone reaches the end of their life, they talk about family more than finances. They discuss relationships more than real estate. And most look for God rather than trying to gain more goods. Keep this at the forefront of your mind as you assess what matters and what doesn't. Life becomes worth living when we invest time and energy into nouns that are living.

39. Your food will get cold if you look at someone else's plate

We all have a lot on our plate. You might start getting hangry (hungry and angry), but I mean this metaphorically. We should give the adequate amount of attention to what's right in front of us. It doesn't take much to lose track of time while scrolling online. Ultimately, this can cost us our lives if we're not paying attention. And I don't know about you, but that's too expensive for me. If we only get one life, why spend it watching everyone else's? This bar reminds me to stop looking at these social media feeds, and focus on taking care of what my life needs.

40. Cultivate it when you're not motivated

The word "cultivate" is not common in our culture. Simply put, it means to make something better. Our goal should be to increase whatever, and whoever we are involved with. If we wait for motivation to begin our elevation, we will find ourselves in procrastination. While all of this rhymes, it's best to use this bar to stop wasting time. If not, we will be left behind. So if you're looking for a reason to get active, this is your sign.

41. If you're not dead, you're not done

I've got good news and bad news for you. The bad news is there's no guarantee you will wake up tomorrow. So many people take their last breath without ever realizing it. On the other hand, the good news is you woke up today. This indicates there's a problem created specifically for you to solve. So don't let what happened yesterday keep you from moving forward today. Your life can be redefined with the endless amount of possibilities that are presented every 24 hours. We should use this bar as fuel to find purpose for every day we're blessed to see.

42. It's not worth it if you're not nervous

Sometimes people use their nerves as a reason not to do something, but I advocate for the exact opposite. Emotions are powerful regardless of how we utilize them. So why not exercise them in a positive way? When we feel nervous, it's not a sign to quit; it's a sign to keep going. Butterflies in your stomach often mean it's time to spread your wings. Oftentimes when we get on the other side of conflict, we can be thankful for an experience we were honestly just excited for. Make sure you're using your feelings instead of letting them use you.

43. The next one is the best one

Athletes often use this bar when explaining how they aren't focusing on the last championship; instead their concentration is geared towards the next one. Whether we consider ourselves athletic or not, we will always have room for improvement in our lives. And if we're not thinking about how to get right, it won't be long before we're getting left. Dr. Myles Munroe always used to say, *"The greatest enemy to progress is your last success"*. The only way we can defeat our enemy is by using our energy to better our "inner me".

"If we're not thinking about how to get right, it won't be long before we're getting left."

44. You grow more when you know more

Squeeze every lesson out of life, and watch how much wiser you become. There is always an individual, instance or incident in history we can gain knowledge from to fuel our greatness. At the same time, let's not get ahead of ourselves. It is important to remember we still have to apply everything we learn. But you deserve props because reading a book like this exemplifies your desire to seek, which will help you reach your peak.

45. Know the end before you begin

Have you ever skipped reading the instruction manual and later said to yourself, "This ain't it"? Well if you haven't, I know for a fact I have. It saves me the stress and mess when I remember following the guide is best. This matters when assembling products, but this bar can also affect your purpose. It's easy for us to get lost when we don't know where we're going. And it's even easier to stop when we don't have a constant reminder of why we started. We should do our research (internally & externally) so we can find our reason. Will everything always go as planned? Of course not. But this is why we should write our plan in pencil, and pen our purpose in permanent marker.

46. "How to" comes from knowing you

You make it through by doing what works best for you. Social media gurus may advertise their methods for success, but we have to find out for ourselves which way is best. I'm not saying they're wrong, but we don't have the brain capacity to listen to everybody. My best recommendation is to stay true to who you are. If you do this, you'll make it further than if you were trying to be someone else.

47. All you have is all you need

In the biblical parable of the talents (Matthew 25:14-30), a man entrusted his goods to three servants. Two of them multiplied what they received. The other one allowed fear to keep them from producing more fruit. In the end, those who did more received more. And the one who did less ended with nothing left. You don't have to be spiritual to understand you're the only person who can make the most out of what you have. The only time we don't feel good enough is when we're not focused on our own stuff. So if we find ourselves stressed, reassess so we can make more progress.

48. Pay attention or the pay the price

Paying attention to detail is imperative to your purpose. It won't be the end of the world if we don't do it in school, but it could end someone's life if we don't do it in the car. Lack of focus can affect our lives and those around us. It is in our best interest to give our undivided attention to whatever is in front of us, so we can leave it behind us.

49. You have not because you ask not

This truth comes straight from Scripture (James 4:2). People may be able to read our handwriting, our lips, or even our social media bios–but they cannot read our minds. If we want something, we must ask for it. Of course, it's important to examine our motives, but the principle still stands. Think about the times you've asked someone what was wrong, and they kept insisting, "nothing". They weren't fooling anyone. In the same way, we look just as unwise when we refuse to speak up for what we truly want in life.

50. Triple AAA plan to overcome mistakes: Admit. Assess. Advance.

You may be familiar with this acronym when it comes to roadside assistance, but it also applies to when we need personal assistance. If we ADMIT we were wrong, we won't live in deception. If we ASSESS what went wrong, it will be easier to do right next time. And when we ADVANCE, we will be thankful for this process so we don't get stuck on the road called "Life".

51. If it ain't broke, don't fix it

You have probably heard this one before, but I promise you'll never hear it enough. If something works, don't try to reinvent the wheel. Greatness is about consistency, doing the same thing well until it becomes second nature. If you get bored, do your best to add nuances to what you're already doing. This will take you further than trying to fix something that was never broken in the first place.

52. If you don't use it, you'll lose it

Every one of us has been blessed with gifts and talents. But they only grow when we put them to work. If we don't, we fail to give responsibilities to our abilities. The best example is working out in the gym. I could build muscle in one season, then lose it in the next—all because I got distracted by the ups and downs of life. Understandable? Sure. Excusable? Never. We are each born with a gift—and only given a limited time to give it.

53. A winner is a loser who kept on trying

For all my sports fans out there, this one's for you. Michael Jordan never lost in the NBA Finals, but his first trip there didn't come until his 7th season. You don't need a calculator to know MJ (arguably the GOAT in basketball) spent far more time losing than he did winning. Yet those losses became fuel, not failure. But when we love what we do, those losses will sharpen us until we finally win again.

54. Every "opp" is an opposition or opportunity

How do you view obstacles in your life? Do they look like roadblocks, or are they stepping stones to your destiny? I guarantee you life will always have something for us to overcome. But our perspective determines if we press forward. Keeping this in mind will give us access to life's greatest rewards. So let's remember our optics are more important than our "opps".

55. Haste makes waste

I don't know about you, but the word "haste" is not in my daily vocabulary. The definition is "excessive speed or urgency of movement or action". This tells me that I'm taking a risk when I'm in a rush. Why? Because I am wasting energy that would serve me better if I slow down, and pay attention to the details. Usually the output is better when I am more attentive to my input (especially when I'm in the kitchen). Hopefully you will learn from my foolishness. Take a second to pause, and properly assess so you can do your best.

56. Seasoning makes everything better

As someone who loves food, I can confirm the validity and value of this bar. But what you may not have realized is the same can be said with the seasons we go through in life. Have you ever experienced a tough time, and been thankful for it when you came out on the other side? Me too. Don't discredit what is guiding you to your destiny. Just like you can tell the difference when food is seasoned, you can tell when someone has gotten better from a season.

57. You can be it even if you don't see it

If there is something we want to be that the world has never heard of, it's probably our purpose to become it. Just because we've yet to see it on a screen, doesn't mean it will never be seen. This often signifies how we can leave our signature touch on life. Creating something from our imagination is the highest form of value we can offer. So if something bothers your brain, find out if it's your gift calling your name.

58. Trust your insight over your eyesight

Studies show that over four billion people around the world wear glasses (I'm proud to be one of them). This alone reminds us how fickle our eyes can be. While sight helps us receive information, insight helps us believe information. And belief is what gives us the courage to keep moving forward, even when what we see looks uncertain. Our understanding should always give us hope to go further than where we're standing.

59. Repairs are easier when you understand how to build

Who really loves going to the mechanic to get their car fixed? Whether your hand is raised or not, the truth is—we need their expertise. Mechanics spend countless hours studying auto parts so they know exactly what to do to get us back on the road. The same is true in life. Relationships, self-care, and personal growth all require the occasional tune-up. But repairs are always easier when we understand the process of building in the first place. If we don't take the time to gain understanding of what we use, we'll run out of options when it's time to choose.

60. It takes all night to become an overnight success

"Overnight success" is a phrase we hear when a celebrity seems to rise to stardom in the blink of an eye. But time will always reveal what's fake and what's real. If what we're doing isn't legit, the fame and fortune won't stick because it was never authentic. What most people don't see are the countless seasons of sacrifice and struggle behind the spotlight. That's why we shouldn't waste our nights comparing our lights.

61. God won't excuse what we don't use

Our motion makes room for miracles. When I realized this, I saw I had two choices: get up or stay stuck. The same 24 hours are given to all of us, and it's our job to utilize each second wisely. As mentioned before, if we don't use it we lose it. That's why it's so important to optimize our time and effort if we want to claim today's prize. After all, we shouldn't ask God to part the Red Sea while we're still sitting in a boat.

62. Working on yourself is better than working on everyone else

Your purpose is an inside job, and you're the only employee. External factors can affect your purpose, but they cannot wreck your purpose. Show me somebody who won while playing the "blame game". Right after, I'll show you how that same person lost the game of life. Our success is our responsibility. It should be our duty to learn from what we go through to get where we want to go to.

"External factors can affect your purpose, but they cannot wreck your purpose."

63. Failure is a key ingredient to success

There is always a secret to any good recipe. If it isn't included, the quality of what we're making would drastically diminish. The same can be said when referring to becoming successful. NBA legend Kobe Bryant is a prime example of this. As an 18-year-old rookie, he air-balled 4 jumpers in a playoff game vs. the Utah Jazz. If he isolated this incident, he wouldn't be remembered as one of the most iconic basketball players ever. We have to view failing with humility so we can fail forward. Once we press past our problem, we are able to perceive how potent failing can be in our winning recipe.

64. No pressure, no progress

When cookies go in the oven, the dough needs to be baked at extreme temperatures to reach the desired outcome. Believe it or not, we are no different. We are pressed with excruciating circumstances so we can be prepared for promotion. When we feel heat, it's important to not confuse it with defeat. As a result, we will be able to serve the world in a greater capacity than if we stayed in the same stage of life we started in.

65. God doesn't need to change the system to change your situation

Every four to eight years, a new president is elected. Whether we like the candidate or not, their time in office is temporary. Just because they're in power doesn't mean they can take away ours. Here's how you can keep it simple: control what you can control. If you don't, life will always feel like it's out of control. Politics may affect us, but they don't have to infect us. Our job is to persevere through the circumstances and still walk in purpose. Over time, when we shift our perspective and renew our minds, we'll see our situation begin to change. Because renewing your mind is just as important as depending on the divine.

66. Just because you could doesn't mean you should

We have free will to do what we please, but we have to decide if it's truly what we need. The greatest enemy to doing something right is doing something good. Good and bad shouldn't be hard to grasp. But deciding between good and right is more of a task. The right thing often prioritizes your end goal. For example, just because I *could* order takeout doesn't mean I *should*. I have to decide if this aligns with my budget. Our destinies demand discipline. A short-term decision may not be worth a long-term result.

67. If you do it fast, it won't last

This one is simple, but it is easier said than done when there are external/internal pressures on us. SLOW DOWN. Take a deep breath and then proceed. More often than not, I find myself doing the same task multiple times because I didn't follow instructions the first time. The best pros master moving slow. Doing the same thing with intention naturally speeds up our ascension. If we rush, we will make mistakes, which can keep us from being great. We should take our time so we can save our time.

"Doing the same thing with intention naturally speeds up our ascension."

HAPPINESS

When you break down the word "happiness", it's easy to find the word "happy". The prefix "hap" "means fortune or chance", while the suffix "-y" means to "be full of". When you put it all together, happiness can be defined as having a feeling everything is working together in your favor. But here's the disclaimer: this will take some work on your behalf. The final section of this book assists us in simplifying happiness, but it is our job to find it. We have to choose daily to turn our attention from what we're stressed with, to focusing on what we're blessed with.

68. Everything that settles is at the bottom

This is one of my favorite bars because it reminds me of how to separate the best from the worst when making a decision. It's better to carry the weight of going after what we want, rather than wishing we did. Hip-Hop rapper J. Cole once said, *"It ain't like life comes often. Only thing worse than death is a regret-filled coffin"*. Those words hit hard because they're true–time is the most important non-renewable resource we have. If we only get to live this life once, we should make it a life worth living.

69. Anything not growing is dead

Aren't you tired of going through the motions? You may also know how stimulating progression can be. Few moments compare to doing something we feel we are born to do. When my reason is bigger than me, it's easier to exert my energy. If there is someone or a situation that isn't helping us grow, we have to become strong enough to say no.

70. What's in you comes out of you

When we're weighed down mentally, it slows us down physically. We can try to bypass it in our brains, but it's harder to ignore it in our behavior. Positivity is no different. When we plant good seeds in our mind, good deeds aren't too far behind. This means we have two choices. We either rehearse it or release it. Controlling the input isn't always feasible, but it's our job to make sure the output is reasonable.

"We either rehearse it or release it."

71. Creative, restorative or lucrative

Adding value to ourselves and others is simplified when we engage in these types of hobbies. Granted, it takes time to figure out which activities are fun and fulfilling. Keep exploring and trust the process. You may think, "What about my other hobbies?" I'm not telling you to stop doing them. I'm here to help you understand how they are beneficial to you. The goal of this bar is to aid us in determining if our interests are doing a number on us, or helping us do numbers.

72. Be yourself, God takes care of everything else

When I focus on everything around me, I forget to be me. But when I am reminded to use my authenticity, a sense of peace surrounds me. God is simple. It is not in His nature to confuse us of who we're supposed to be (1 Corinthians 14:33). Anything that contradicts or distracts us from fulfilling our purpose does not have our best interest in mind. So be yourself. Besides, everyone else is already taken.

73. You run into what you're running from

Every time I wash clothes, I notice how much I love graphic t-shirts and hate folding laundry. Sometimes I pretend like this conflict doesn't exist, but eventually I have to dig through a heap of garments to find what I'm looking for. Moral of the story: it's better to do it now than waiting around. Whether it's motion or emotion, neither are fixed by some magic potion. If you're looking for something to run to, make sure you find a better version of you.

74. Focus on gaining, not complaining

Complaining is such an easy thing to do, hence why many people do it. I'm not exempt from this and you probably aren't either. Gaining requires perseverance and perspiration, which is why only a few people do it. Life is constantly giving us experiences to use for extraction or distraction. It's up to us to decide if we move on or continue to think wrong. Which one will you choose? Where we let our focus go, dictates what will grow.

75. Your belief affects your behavior

You can't convince me that Kobe Bryant isn't the greatest basketball player of all time. Now, this isn't to start a debate

—it's just to illustrate. I even mimic his basketball moves around the house. From his footwork to free throw, you name it. As funny as that may sound, it proves a point: we often behave how we believe, even unconsciously. The key is alignment. When our beliefs and behaviors match, it becomes easier to achieve what we believe.

76. Intention follows your attention

Our presence is the greatest present we can present to someone. There is something special about knowing we have someone's undivided attention. It's easy to let electronics steal the spotlight from these interactions, but what if we make it our sole intent to be right where we are? Not only do we become more useful, but our relationships become more fruitful. Let's pay attention to what/who purifies our intentions.

77. What's for you will never ignore you

Whoever said hindsight is 20/20 wasn't lying. There have been people and opportunities that didn't want me, despite me wanting them. I eventually understood divine redirection can be disguised as rejection. Finding what contributes to your calling is no different. Certain things will continue to nag until we add it to our bag. We have to learn to discern what our destiny demands. After reading this book, I hope you begin to pour more into what your purpose won't ignore.

78. You won't heal until you reveal

As we go through life, experiences will shape who we are without us realizing it. However, there are also moments when we are fully aware of what we're holding onto (even if it hinders us). The only way to move on is to get what's inside of you outside of you. Share what's bothering you with a loved one, friend or even a therapist. We're more likely to feel better when we stop walking around with what is weighing us down.

> *"The only way to move on is to get what's inside of you outside of you."*

79. Subtract what's not adding to your life

Can I tell you a secret? I unashamedly don't remember most of what I learned in school as an adolescent.

Thankfully this math concept is an easy one to grasp. Adding is used for more, while subtraction takes away what's not necessary to our core. This logic can be applied to money, food ingredients or even relationships. When we realize something or someone isn't adding to our joy, peace or wallet we need to subtract it.

80. You can't give something you ain't got

This bar becomes crucial when using the "F word". No, not that one. I'm referring to when we need to say, *"I forgive you"*. It became easier for me to forgive others after I forgave myself. Happiness can't do what it does when we hesitate to show love. Let's be intentional with taking the time to forgive ourselves, so we can pass this blessing on to everyone else.

81. Peace shouldn't have a price tag

Weighing options becomes simplified when utilizing this bar. Certain opportunities would've made me more money, but would've caused me more madness if I accepted them. Some relationships would've ruined me if I didn't refuse to be misused. In these moments, we should always choose peace instead of chasing pleasure. If it costs us our peace, it's too expensive.

82. You get pressed before you get blessed

This sucks to say aloud, but it's more normal than you may think. Flowers cannot grow without rain and dirt, similar to how we won't find true happiness avoiding pain and hurt. We have to appreciate the winter as much as we enjoy the summer. It's easy to whine when we don't shine, but we gain clarity when it's our time. So let's make note of every way we're being pressed, because this is a part of the journey to being blessed.

> *"It's easy to whine when we don't shine, but we gain clarity when it's our time."*

83. You can lose weight and still be heavy

We can go to the gym, eat healthy, see a doctor regularly and still walk around feeling weighed down. A lot of times we are holding onto grudges, past traumas and regret. The truth is these all would serve us better if we just let them go. Easier said than done, but it's the first step to making sure the mental battle is won. If we don't work from the inside out, our life will feel like it's upside down. Let's choose to be lighthearted instead of heavy-laden.

84. A little & a lot depends on what you got

Compare eating grapes to munching on potato chips. Without question, the former is deemed healthier than the latter. And it's no coincidence fruit will cure our hunger quicker than processed food can. We can assess life with this same perspective. There isn't enough sex, money or drugs to satisfy our souls. Choosing to attract instead of chase ensures our hearts and minds are in the right place.

85. Count your blessings, not your likes

It's easy to get lost in the analytics of social media. Businesses use these numbers to scale, but if this is how we measure our worth we'll fail. The average content creator may find it impossible to go viral every post. This is why counting blessings instead of likes is a better reason to boast. This bar is a reminder to focus on value instead of volume. Sidebar: most of our "likes" come from people who never truly liked us.

"Businesses use these numbers to scale, but if this is how we measure our worth we'll fail."

86. There's less stress when we do our best

We're at the point where we can say this in unison: control what you can control. We have to trust everything will work out in our favor. Falling victim to pressure will have us thinking otherwise. Self-awareness and maturity helps us realize we can only do so much. And if we try to do too much, we won't have much left. Focus on doing your best, and being at peace with the rest.

87. Live your life, don't let it live you

Punching the clock and paying bills can feel like walking up a never-ending hill. There's nothing wrong with this life, but getting lost in it never seems right. If we are not living well, each day will lead us into feeling stale. It's best to prioritize what keeps our lives fresh. From time to time we will need a vacation, but life is better when we choose the right vocation.

88. Find humility before it finds you

The root word in humility is "humi", which refers to something that comes from the ground. Oftentimes this is exactly where people who are prideful fall. We will never be too good to learn from the people around us. On the other hand, being humble can be misconstrued. Humbling ourselves means knowing the difference between confidence and arrogance. We shouldn't have to compare ourselves to others to know who we are. If we forget this bar, the chances are slim for us to make it far.

> "We shouldn't have to compare ourselves to others to know who we are."

89. Go within or go without

Nothing will change until we do. And more often than not, we won't see what we desire until we take ourselves higher. Peace is a great example of a fruit we should look to cultivate daily. If we want peace around us, we have to first find it inside of us. This may include meditation, prayer or any other internal exercise. Do whatever floats your boat, before you feel like you're sinking. We have to take the time to go within so we can win.

90. It's in me not on me

There are people who get complimented on their outfit, and others who wish they had more clothes to complete an outfit. Which one are you? Wherever you find yourself, the principle remains the same. Despite us looking fly, what will be said about us when we die? Without who we are, our attire is incapable of taking us far. If all we think about is wearing designer, we have majored in something minor. How we handle our heart and hands is far greater than wearing name brands.

91. Clearing your mind works every time

The bigger picture doesn't stand a chance when we're too close to our circumstance. This is why vacations are necessary for our wellbeing. It's refreshing to get away, but don't let this time go to waste. If we do this right, we won't have to depend on catching a flight. Some good practices that can be done anywhere are journaling, appreciating nature or even sleeping. It's always easier to reconnect after we reset.

92. Being you gets you through

We will never make it by faking it. There's only one way to find the power to press through: be you. The stresses of life can distract us from properly handling ourselves and others. Problems seem impossible to solve when we are not authentically involved. Knowing who we are can take us very far. "Live, Laugh, Love" might be cliché, but these three things are easier to do when you stay true to being you.

93. If you wanna win, get you a laugh in

There's a time and place for everything, but life is always better when we're laughing. Reading the room is important, but the people in the room usually want to smile and have a good time. Ask yourself this question when your life is filled with strife, *"When was the last time I had a good laugh?"*. I'm not talking about a chuckle or giggle either. Remaining light-hearted helps us get our wins started. "A merry heart does good like medicine, but a broken spirit dries the bones" (Proverbs 17:22).

94. God only fits in where you let Him in

Finding time to pray can be challenging to do every day. Obligations and opportunities can make us believe time is our opponent. The good news is God will help us win every battle we're in. This is why relevant advice can be so divine. But how can we know God's voice if we never give Him our time? God is a gentleman. He will not come into our lives until we let Him in. If we start our days with Him, we won't have to live life on a whim.

95. Getting stuck in the past cancels the future fast

Driving a car while looking in the rearview mirror is an accident waiting to happen. Now imagine this vehicle as a metaphor for your life. It's hard to move forward if our thinking is backwards. There's nothing wrong with reflection, but too much will cause a mental infection. Our minds are not meant to focus on what's behind. Let's move on so we can continue to move up.

96. What you're in won't be where you end

Pretending to always be positive is fool's gold. On the other hand, constant negativity isn't attractive either. Remaining positive is the way to be, but not to the point where we become naive. And if we're always thinking about the bad, how can we expect to see the good? Balance between the two is found when our transparency is sound. This perspective check is easier to handle than a reality check. Being honest with ourselves helps us be hopeful about everything else.

97. We won't heal if we let it build

We'll stay the same if we always play the blame game. It is our job and no one else's to handle what's happening internally. Failure to do this will make our problems multiply, while leaving us divided. Try talking to a trusted source to help you stay the course. Doing this will ensure our problems dissipate instead of accumulate. Even if we don't say it in our native language, how we feel shows up in our body language. Remember, healing comes after revealing.

98. Be content before making content

Burnout is inevitable when we aren't on fire about who we are. Seeking approval through apps on our phones will leave us upset and filled with regret. I'm guilty of making a video despite my heart telling me no. As I matured, I understood this was an attempt to become content. My advice to you would be set boundaries with yourself. Not everything needs to be socially verified in order for it to be a prize. The sooner we see true happiness as fruit of a healthy mind, the better we will present ourselves online.

99. Fill your tanks with thanks

We are guaranteed to experience fatigue on the road to riches. But just like a car needs gas to go, our lives need gratitude to grow. The best way for us to refuel is by seizing every opportunity to say "thank you". It may sound silly, but you'd be surprised how this small phrase can lead to a big change. If we keep the attitude of gratitude, we will maximize our aptitude.

100. Don't make it to the other side without enjoying the ride

What's the point of life if we aren't having fun living it? After all, no one can enjoy it for us. Hardship will come regardless, so there's no need to walk around with a hardened heart. Loosen up. Give grace to yourself and others. The most important question I ask people is, *"Have you smiled today?"*. What should be elementary to our existence often becomes an afterthought. We will be pleased with the culmination of our journeys when we allow joy to guide each step.

If you find a reason to smile, living will be worthwhile.

EPILOGUE

You made it! All 100 of these bars were designed to simplify every step you take and every move you make. Remember: simple doesn't mean easy–there's still work to be done.

Yes, this book had a lot of rhymes, but hopefully that makes it easier to remember at the right time. I've never claimed to be a hip-hop rapper; however, this book is a gift I personally wrapped just for you.

We may never get the pleasure of meeting each other, but thank you for connecting with me through this piece of literature. Each page was written for both motivation **and** application to help you overcome any situation. God bless.

– PERRY RANDLE III

ABOUT THE AUTHOR

Perry Randle III is an established content creator from Kansas City, Missouri. He is unashamed to express his love for Jesus Christ, basketball and pro-wrestling.

Throughout his career, he's had the honor of serving his gift while working with the NBA, WarnerMedia and various other world-renowned media outlets.

After being diagnosed as legally blind in his right eye, Perry's life mantra became ***"Vision Over Sight"***. This motto continues to inspire both himself and others to believe that life can be more than what we see.

www.ingramcontent.com/pod-product-compliance
Lightning Source LLC
Chambersburg PA
CBHW050656160426
43194CB00010B/1959